B   Brown, Fern G.
EAR
HART   Amelia Earhart takes
       off

DATE			
FEB 26	MAY 12		
OCT 16 '88	MAY 19		
DEC 4 '88			
DEC 11 '86			
JAN. 12			
2 10			
MAR 14			
MAR 24			
APR 12			
MAR 24			
APR 29			

© THE BAKER & TAYLOR CO.

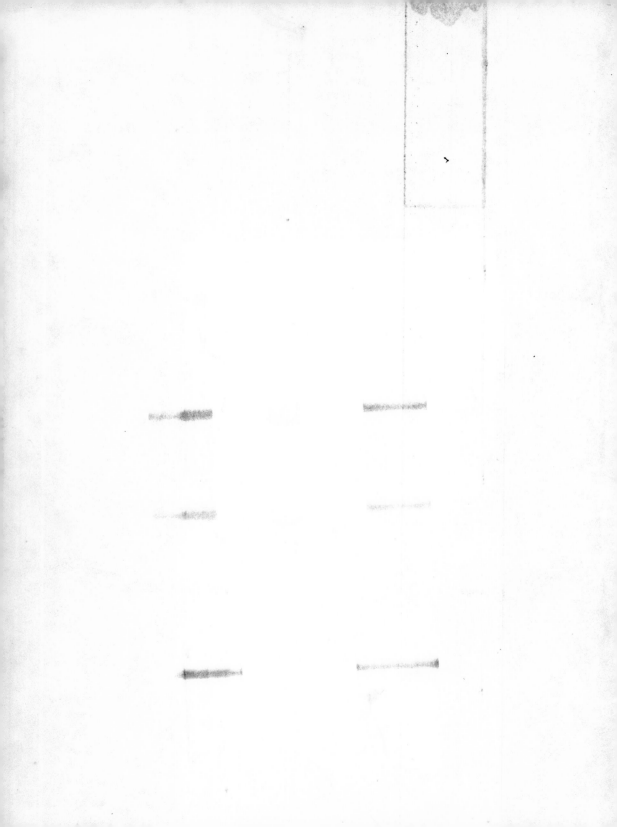

Amelia Earhart Takes Off

FERN G. BROWN

Illustrated by LYDIA HALVERSON

ALBERT WHITMAN & COMPANY, NILES, ILLINOIS

To Marni and Blaine, with love.

The author wishes to thank the following for help with this book: George Priester and Esther E. Noffke of Pal-Waukee Airport, Wheeling, Illinois; Sally Strempl, Marni Debra Brown, and Blaine Parker Barnett.

Library of Congress Cataloging in Publication Data

Brown, Fern G.
    Amelia Earhart takes off.

    Summary: Describes the life of the first woman to fly
solo across the Atlantic, from her adventurous girlhood
to her mysterious disappearance during a flight around
the world in 1937.
    1. Earhart, Amelia, 1897-1937—Juvenile literature.
2. Air pilots—United States—Biography—Juvenile
literature. [1. Earhart, Amelia, 1897-1937. 2. Air
pilots] I. Halverson, Lydia, ill. II. Title.
TL540.E3B74   1985   629.13′092′4   [B]   [92]   85-712
ISBN 0-8075-0309-6

Text © 1985 by Fern G. Brown
Illustrations © 1985 by Albert Whitman & Company
Published in 1985 by Albert Whitman & Company, Niles, Illinois
Published simultaneously in Canada by General Publishing, Limited, Toronto
10   9   8   7   6   5   4   3   2   1

Contents

1 Lively Amelia

When you look up into the sky and see an airplane, think of Amelia Earhart. She was the first woman to fly across the Atlantic Ocean alone. She was the first person to solo between Hawaii and California. Amelia set many other records and changed forever the world's opinion of women as pilots.

Amelia Mary Earhart was the oldest child of Amy Otis Earhart and Edwin Stanton Earhart. She was born in Atchison, Kansas, on July 24, 1897, in her grandparents' home. Her sister, Muriel, was born three years later.

When Amelia was a child, most girls were brought up to be quiet and ladylike. They wore dresses instead of jeans. They played indoors with dolls and toys and learned to sew. But Amelia, often called Millie or Melia, led an active outdoor life.

Unlike most mothers in those days, Mrs. Earhart felt girls should be free to run and play as easily as boys. She often dressed her daughters in blue-flannel gym suits with baggy bloomers. On Saturdays, wearing her gym suit, Amelia rode her bicycle, explored caves, and played tennis and basketball.

A thin-faced child with short, curly blonde hair, Amelia was lively and full of energy. She would run home from school and jump the fence at her grandmother's house instead of using the gate. That worried her grandmother, who thought girls would hurt themselves if they were too physically active. "You don't realize," her grandmother told Amelia one day, "that when I was a small girl I did nothing more strenuous than roll my hoop in the public square." Amelia felt so unladylike she went around by the gate for a few days, but soon she was back to her old habit of jumping the fence.

Amelia's father was a lawyer who worked for the railroad. His salary depended on the cases he won, so the family was never sure of how much money he would make. Often Mr. Earhart had to travel for his job, and most of the time his wife went with him. Because their parents were away so much and to save money, Amelia and Muriel lived in Atchison with their mother's parents during the school year. In summer the four Earharts lived together in Kansas City.

Amelia was good at thinking up interesting things to do. She liked to take chances. It never bothered her if she didn't know how things would turn out. When she was seven years old, she talked her sister, Muriel, and a neighbor, Ralphie Martin, into building a roller coaster. She had seen one at the World's Fair in St. Louis. The children made tracks out of boards and other scraps of lumber. Then they nailed the tracks to the top of a backyard shed roof. The tracks ran down the steep slope of the shed roof and stopped at the ground. Amelia greased them with lard to make them slippery. Next, Amelia, Muriel, and Ralphie made a cart out of a board and four old rollerskate wheels.

Of course, Amelia was the first to try the roller coaster. Using the kitchen stepladder, she climbed to the top of the shed. She might have been scared, but she wouldn't admit it. She climbed into the cart and zoomed down the steep tracks. The skate wheels wobbled and screeched. Suddenly the tracks ended. Amelia and the cart hit the ground with a loud thud. Crash landing!

Some people would have given up. Amelia Earhart didn't, even though her lip was bruised and her dress torn. As soon as she caught her breath she figured out why the roller coaster had crashed. There wasn't enough track running along the ground.

Amelia told her playmates what to do. They weren't so sure she was right, but they were willing to try. With hammers and nails they worked hard fixing the tracks. But the next time Amelia rode the roller coaster, it crashed again. She still wouldn't give up. She fixed the broken parts and added more track on the ground.

Amelia climbed onto the cart at the top of the shed for one last try. Muriel and Ralphie held their breath. Would she make it now? The cart screeched down the tracks. It sounded pretty awful.

This time the cart reached the ground, sailed over the new track, and landed safely. "It's just like flying!" Amelia cried.

Everyone took turns riding the roller coaster. It was great fun. Then Mrs. Earhart found out about it. Fearing someone might get hurt, she told a handyman to take the roller coaster apart. Amelia cried when she saw the pile of boards that had been her wonderful roller coaster. But it probably wasn't long before she thought up another project. She liked to make things happen.

In their grandmother's barn, Amelia, Muriel, and their cousins made up a game they called "Bogie." Sitting in an old abandoned carriage, they studied maps and took imaginary journeys to faraway places. To make the game more exciting, they imagined shadowy creatures hiding in the dark

corners of the haymow. When she was grown-up, Amelia said that her childhood game of map-traveling was like ground-flying an airplane.

Amelia's parents were happy that she was creative and imaginative. They liked her spirit of adventure and urged her to try new things. They wanted her to know and enjoy the outdoors. Sometimes Mr. Earhart took his daughters fishing or for a walk in the woods. Amelia and Muriel collected frogs and insects. Their treasures were kept in a "museum" on the porch. No visitor could enter the house without first being shown the girls' collection.

Amelia's father bought his daughters guns, bats, baseballs, and footballs. He encouraged them to try all kinds of sports that boys usually played. The Christmas of 1905, when Amelia was eight years old, Mr. Earhart gave Amelia and Muriel boys' bellywhopper sleds with steel runners. These sleds were built close to the ground, and you went downhill on your belly.

Amelia's old sled had wooden runners. She had to sit up straight on it, and it must have seemed as slow as a turtle. What she liked most about her new sled was its speed. She loved to hear the swishing sound of the steel runners whizzing through the snow.

One day, after a heavy snowfall, Amelia went sledding at a nearby hill. She bellyflopped onto her new sled. Just as she took off, a junkman with his horse and cart rounded the curve at the bottom of the hill. Amelia shouted to get the man's attention, but he didn't hear her. She was going a mile a minute. They were bound to crash.

Amelia thought fast. Holding the sled tightly, she aimed it between the horse's front and hind legs. She squeezed her eyes shut. When she opened them again, she'd passed under the horse's stomach—without a scratch!

Amelia liked all animals. When she was little, she even took a wooden donkey instead of a doll to bed with her at night. She was especially fond

of horses, but her grandmother wouldn't let her ride. She was afraid a horse might run away with her precious granddaughter. It wasn't until Amelia was grown-up that she took riding lessons. As an adult, horseback riding was probably her favorite sport, but she also enjoyed tennis and swimming.

Although Amelia was an outdoor person, she loved books, too. Mrs. Earhart often read to her young daughters before they went to sleep. When the girls were older, everyone in the family took turns reading aloud. Many times while Amelia did the dishes, Muriel would sit at the kitchen table and read to her. When it was Muriel's turn to work, Amelia would read aloud. The sisters particularly liked poetry. They often recited their favorite poems while they swept the floor, following the rhythm with their brooms.

Amelia's father wanted his children to know what was going on in the world. Since 1903, when the Wright brothers had flown the first airplane at Kitty Hawk, North Carolina, there had been great interest in aviation. Men flew in any craft they could get into the air. In those days, however, most people believed that no respectable woman would fly.

On Amelia's eleventh birthday, Mr. Earhart took his daughters to the Iowa State Fair to see a plane fly. To Amelia, it looked like a big old wooden crate tied together with rusty wire.

The pilot, wearing goggles, sat between the two wings. His feet were on a crossbar. There was a propeller in back of the plane. Amelia watched a mechanic spin the propeller around and around. It made a loud, whirring sound and blew dust all over the field. She wiped her face with her handkerchief. The motor started to sputter. Slowly, very slowly, the small wheels inched forward. Then the plane picked up speed and left the ground.

Mr. Earhart waved his hat as the plane lurched into the air. But Amelia didn't give the funny boxy thing a second glance. She tugged at her father's sleeve. There were cows and horses to see that were much more interesting.

In 1907 Mr. Earhart was put on a regular salary by the Rock Island Railroad. This meant he would make enough money to have his family with him winter and summer. That was good news for the Earharts. Amelia and Muriel went to Des Moines, Iowa, to live permanently with their parents.

Amelia missed her grandparents and playmates in Atchison, but she was happy that her family was together all the time. Now when her parents traveled on business, she and Muriel went along. For Amelia each trip was an exciting adventure. It was the most fun when the Earharts lived in a private railroad car. Sometimes, when the train stopped in Atchison, Amelia's grandmother would come aboard to share a meal with them. Although the girls often had to miss school to go with their parents, Amelia thought she learned just as much traveling as she would have in a classroom.

At first everything went well for the Earharts in Des Moines, but after a while Mr. Earhart found his job boring and began to drink, often neglecting his work. The family called his drinking problem "Dad's sickness," and they never spoke of it in public.

Mr. Earhart was usually a kind, caring, generous parent. Amelia loved him for many things, especially his sense of humor. But his drinking made her sad and angry. One day while she was packing her father's suitcase for a business trip, she found a bottle of whiskey hidden among his socks. She opened the bottle and poured the whiskey down the sink. Just then her father came into the kitchen. When he saw what Amelia had done, he was so angry he was ready to hit her. Luckily, her mother came in and calmed him. Later he apologized to his daughter, and on that trip at least, left his liquor home.

Amelia must have soon realized that there was nothing she or anyone else could do to keep her father from alcohol. When she was grown-up, she understood his drinking was an illness. Being a strong, responsible person, she tried to take care of her mother and sister. She frequently sent them clothing and money and was so concerned about the details of their lives that at times she might have seemed meddlesome and bossy.

Because of his drinking, Mr. Earhart lost his job in Des Moines. He went away for a month to get over his "sickness." When he returned he promised he would never again touch a drop of liquor.

11

Amelia's grandmother died in 1911. It was the custom then for the man of the family to handle the finances. But because she thought her son-in-law could not take care of money, she stated in her will that Amelia's mother would not inherit anything for twenty years or until Mr. Earhart was dead. Mr. Earhart was so enraged by his mother-in-law's will that he began to drink again, even more than before. The next two years must have been miserable for everyone in the family. Amelia and Muriel and their parents moved again and again while Mr. Earhart tried to hold down a job. At last Mr. and Mrs. Earhart decided to separate. Mr. Earhart went to Kansas City to live with his sister and her family. The railroad wouldn't rehire him because of his drinking, so he opened his own law office there. Mrs. Earhart took the girls to Chicago to live with friends.

Four years was the most the Earharts ever lived in one place. Maybe that's why Amelia never felt that she had a real home anywhere. She said once that when people greeted her by saying, "I'm from your home town," she had to ask, "Which one?"

Because they moved so often, Amelia and Muriel didn't make many good friends. But they did learn to get along with all kinds of people. Later, when Amelia became famous, she found it easy to meet and talk to strangers. She thought it probably was because she'd lived in so many places as a child.

Amelia went to six high schools, but it took her only four years to get a diploma. She was graduated in June 1915 from Hyde Park High School in Chicago. The caption under Amelia's photo in the class yearbook was an accurate prediction of the future. It said, "The girl in brown who walks alone." Amelia was a loner, and she always preferred flying alone.

After Amelia's graduation, Mrs. Earhart and the girls moved back to Kansas City to live with Mr. Earhart. The Earharts needed money to send the girls to college. Mrs. Earhart's inheritance had been badly managed by her brother, and only part of it was left. In the fall of 1916, persuaded by her husband, Mrs. Earhart went to court and broke her mother's will. She received the remainder of her money and was able to send Muriel to St. Margaret's College in Toronto, Canada, and Amelia to Ogontz, a girls' boarding school near Philadelphia, Pennsylvania.

Amelia was happy to leave home and go to school. Although her father had stopped drinking, Mr. and Mrs. Earhart were not getting along. While the girls were away, their mother and father spent more and more time apart.

In the fall of 1917, Mrs. Earhart was living alone in an apartment hotel in Toronto near Muriel's school when Amelia went to join her mother and sister for the Christmas holidays. It was bitterly cold as Amelia hurried down the street to meet Muriel. She drew her scarf tightly around her neck. Turning the corner, she saw four soldiers coming toward her. Canada had been fighting in World War I for three years. Every single one of the men approaching had lost a leg! As the men passed, tears filled Amelia's eyes. Her heart ached for the handicapped soldiers—for all soldiers. They had given so much to the war.

It took Amelia only a minute to make up her mind. School suddenly seemed unimportant to her. She felt she couldn't spend time studying when so many men were suffering. She told her mother she wanted to stay in Toronto and help in the hospitals.

Amelia was persuaded to go back to school, but within two months she had her mother's permission to return to Toronto to nurse the wounded. She took a special Canadian Red Cross course, and when it was completed, she became a nurse's aide at Spadina Military Hospital. Many young men there were ill with influenza (as a result of the terrible epidemic that broke out in 1918) or had been wounded in the war. Amelia quickly grew to hate war. All through her life, whenever she had the chance, she spoke out for peace.

Being a nurse's aide made Amelia feel useful. In her gray-and-white uniform, she worked hard twelve hours a day. She had only two hours off in the afternoon. She made beds, scrubbed floors, carried trays of food, and gave out medicine. Life for the men in the hospital was a little better because of Amelia Earhart.

During her spare time, she often visited with Muriel. One day a friend who was a flyer in the Royal Flying Corps invited the sisters to watch him do some stunts. He skimmed out over the field and put the plane into a loop. He made one graceful turn, then another. When the plane plunged into a low dive, Amelia felt a thrill of excitement. From then on, airplanes began to interest her. Whenever she had free time, she would go to a flying field and watch the soldiers who were learning to fly.

One snowy November day, Amelia saw a training plane take off on skiis. She barely felt the stinging snow blown by the propellers. Suddenly she knew she wanted to fly. Now! Quickly she ran to ask permission to go for a ride from the officer in charge. But she was turned down. Not even the general's wife could fly in a military plane, he told her.

No matter how busy Amelia was at the hospital, she couldn't stop thinking about the "devil flying machine." When she went to a flying field, she spent her time talking with the pilots about aviation. They teased her and said she was "ground-flying." The teasing didn't bother Amelia. She was learning a lot.

But as much as she liked to talk about airplanes, she didn't plan to ground-fly forever. She wanted to know what flying was really like. She didn't know when or how she'd find out, but she knew she would. Amelia Earhart always made things happen, didn't she?

2 Amelia Takes Off

When the war was over, Amelia planned to begin studying medicine, but she became ill with a severe sinus infection. Today, antibiotics would probably have cured it, but because they were not available then Amelia had to have surgery. She spent the spring of 1919 with her mother and sister in Northampton, Massachusetts, recuperating from the operation.

While Muriel attended Smith College, in Northampton, Amelia, who was not well enough to go to school full time, took banjo lessons and a course in automobile-engine repair. When school was out, Mrs. Earhart and the girls spent a relaxing summer at Lake George where Amelia slowly regained her health and strength.

In the fall Amelia enrolled at Columbia University, and her mother went to New York to help get her settled. Eagerly Amelia started her premedical courses, but in a very short time, she realized she wouldn't make a good doctor. She didn't like the idea of sometimes having to deal with people's imaginary illnesses. Medical research would be a much better career for her, she decided.

In April 1920, Amelia's plans changed again. Her mother needed minor surgery, and Amelia advised her to have it done in California. Mr. Earhart was living in Los Angeles, and he wanted his family with him again. He had given up drinking and become a Christian Scientist. Amelia and Muriel promised they would follow their mother to Los Angeles, and Mrs. Earhart agreed to go.

When school was out, Amelia joined her parents in Los Angeles where her father had opened a law office. She intended to return to New York later and continue her studies in medical research.

In California in the 1920s, men who had been pilots during the war were putting on shows called air circuses. Amelia liked to watch the fliers do stunts with their planes. Once she went with her father to an air circus in Long Beach. The little planes dived and looped and turned in the sky. Amelia couldn't take her eyes off them. She was just as fascinated by flying as she had been in Toronto. She asked her father to find out how long it would take to learn to fly and how much lessons cost. A pilot told Mr. Earhart that it only took five to ten hours to learn, but that lessons cost a thousand dollars!

In 1920 a thousand dollars was a lot of money, about the same as ten thousand dollars is today. Amelia knew her father couldn't afford to give her flying lessons. When Mr. Earhart asked why she wanted to know about lessons, Amelia told him she wasn't sure. She didn't fool her father. He could tell that she really wanted to fly.

Because he always encouraged her to try new things, Mr. Earhart arranged for Amelia to be a passenger on an airplane. It wasn't the same as taking lessons, but it didn't cost a thousand dollars, either. The price was only one dollar for ten minutes.

On a beautiful summer day in 1920, Amelia and her father went to Rogers Airport, a big, open field on Wilshire Boulevard surrounded by oil wells. The pilot was a famous flyer named Frank Hawks.

"As soon as we left the ground, I knew I myself had to fly," Amelia wrote later. There was no feeling of speed, but in just a few seconds, she saw the ocean down below and recognized the Hollywood Hills in the distance. Amelia's heart soared with the plane. Nothing on earth had ever made her feel so happy and free.

Amelia told her parents she wanted to learn to fly. She said later, "I

17

knew full well I'd die if I didn't." When her father said he couldn't afford to pay for lessons, Amelia was very disappointed, but she wouldn't give up. If her father couldn't help her, she would earn the money somehow.

She found a good pilot who agreed to be her teacher. The pilot's name was Neta Snook, but everyone called her Snooky. To pay for the lessons, Amelia worked at several odd jobs. Her first was at the telephone company. Later she worked for a photography studio. The jobs paid little for the long hours she put in. But she managed to save, and she took a lesson whenever she had enough money. Snooky did not charge her for ground instruction, only for instruction in the air.

On weekends, Amelia was always at the airport. She was a good mechanic and sometimes helped fix broken engines. Her parents scarcely saw her now.

At first Snooky taught Amelia about the airplane and all its parts. Then lessons began in the air. In Snooky's plane there were two open cockpits, each with the same controls and instruments. When Amelia and Snooky flew, Amelia sat in the front cockpit. If she made a mistake, Snooky could correct it. When teacher and pupil wanted to talk to each other, they had to yell because the plane was so noisy.

There were many plane crashes in those early days of aviation. Amelia's first crash came with Snooky at the controls. They were about fifty feet off the ground when the engine failed during takeoff. Snooky turned off the ignition, and they bounced down in a cabbage field. It seemed as if the plane might tip over, but Amelia stayed calm and climbed out with only a slight injury to her tongue. Amelia enjoyed flying so much that accidents didn't faze her. She called them the "flat tires of flying." She was always calm, which may be one reason she lived through ten plane crashes.

Later, when Snooky sold her plane, Amelia took advanced lessons from John Montijo, an expert flying teacher. Amelia worked hard on the

ground and in the sky. But it was a while before the other flyers thought of her as an equal. She had to prove herself many times. When the men got to know her better, they admired her courage and independence. They said Amelia Earhart was a "natural" pilot.

Amelia at twenty-three was a tall, slim young woman. She was not considered beautiful, but she had good features. People especially liked her warm blue-gray eyes. Friends thought she had charm, self-confidence, and a quiet sense of humor.

In the days of dirt runways, airfields were dusty. Male flyers dressed in old military clothes. Amelia wore the same kind of khaki pants, leather coat, and boots that the men did. She didn't want to look different. Secretly she began to clip off her hair, a little at a time. She was afraid to cut it really short for fear people might think she was odd.

By 1921, Amelia had flown about ten hours. Because she had to earn the money for the lessons it had taken almost six months, but now she was ready to solo.

On the day she was to fly alone, Snooky and Muriel and several others watched as Amelia climbed into the cockpit. She wasn't a bit nervous as she buckled her helmet and pulled the goggles over her eyes. She taxied to the end of the runway and checked her controls and instruments. Everything was in order.

Amelia opened the throttle and the plane started down the runway. Then she felt a wing sag. She didn't panic but calmly brought the plane to a stop. When she climbed out, mechanics and other pilots ran toward her. The plane was pushed back to the hangar for repairs.

Someone else might have put off soloing that day, but Amelia wouldn't hear of it. As soon as the repairs were made, she climbed back into the pilot's seat. After a perfect takeoff, she went up to five thousand feet. Alone in the sky, Amelia experienced the joyous, free feeling that flying always gave her.

On their first solo flight, many pilots stay up in the air a long time because they are afraid to land. But Amelia wasn't frightened. She went up to five thousand feet, flew around Los Angeles, and calmly prepared to land. When she was almost at ground level, she pulled up the airplane's nose and waited for a smooth landing. Instead, the plane banged onto the ground and a second later bounced back into the air. Amelia had forgotten to reduce the engine power!

Quickly, she pulled the throttle to idle and eased the stick back as far as it would go. Down went the plane again. This time it landed, hitting the ground with a loud thump.

Snooky and Muriel were glad to see the plane safely down. They thought Amelia might have been afraid, but she was only disappointed in her skill as a pilot. "I felt silly," she said later. "My first solo had come and gone without anything to mark it but an exceptionally poor landing."

Amelia promised herself that she would practice even more. She wanted to be an expert pilot.

Amelia liked to go up in the air alone. Because the other flyers teased her about this, she sometimes practiced at a flying field where nobody knew her.

Her hard work paid off. A year later Amelia earned the only kind of pilot's license in existence, the Fédération Aéronautique Internationale. Today every pilot must earn a license in accordance with the rules of the Federal Aviation Authority. But in the early days of aviation, it wasn't necessary to have a license. People just flew when and if they could. Amelia wanted her license to prove that she was officially qualified to fly.

On Amelia's twenty-fifth birthday, July 24, 1922, she bought a used yellow sports plane from W. G. Kinner, the owner of the airfield where she took flying lessons. Amelia liked the plane even though experienced pilots told her it was too light and didn't have enough engine power. She paid Kinner what money she had in her savings account. To earn the rest, she took a job driving a truck for a sand-and-gravel company.

Mrs. Earhart didn't want her daughter driving a truck, so she and Muriel paid off Amelia's debt. In return, Amelia promised to spend more time at home, which she tried to do. Mr. Earhart wasn't enthusiastic about Amelia owning a plane. He thought that airplanes were unsafe, and he wouldn't ride in them. But Mrs. Earhart fully supported Amelia's desire to fly. She said later she felt flying was something her daughter had to do. Although Amelia was in many crashes, Mrs. Earhart said she didn't worry because she trusted her daughter's judgment.

Amelia soon found that owning an airplane cost a great deal of money. To cut expenses, she let Kinner use the plane, and in return he gave her free hangar space. Nobody was more pleased and proud to own a plane than Amelia. She enjoyed practicing stunt flying. She learned stalls, rolls, and skids and how to put a plane into a tailspin and pull it out.

During an air meet in October, Amelia asked an official of the California Aero Club to seal a barograph in her plane. A barograph is an instrument that records how high a plane has flown. Her sister and father watched as she took off. An hour later, when Amelia landed, the seal was opened. She had climbed to fourteen thousand feet. Although men in bigger planes had gone higher, Amelia had set a new women's altitude record. It was her first record.

After a while, Amelia sold her little yellow plane and bought a new Kinner model. She had helped Kinner work on the engine. Amelia was proud of her new plane. She wanted to fly to Boston, where Muriel was now teaching English, and show it off. But once again, family problems forced her to change her plans. In 1924 Mr. and Mrs. Earhart's twenty-nine-year marriage ended in divorce. Mrs. Earhart decided to move to Boston to join Muriel while Mr. Earhart would remain in California.

By now Amelia must have realized that just as she couldn't stop her father from drinking, there was nothing she could do to force her parents to be happy together. She loved them both but decided to make her home near Boston with her mother and sister.

Amelia sold her plane and bought a car. She drove her mother to Boston, and the three women found a place to live near where Muriel was teaching. Within a week after they arrived, Amelia had another sinus operation to relieve the condition she'd had since the war.

When Amelia recovered from surgery, she attended pre-med classes at Columbia for a short time. Her first love was still flying, but she thought of it only as a hobby, as most people did in those days. She had to find another way to earn money. Although she was still interested in medicine, she finally decided against a medical career. In the fall of 1925, when she was twenty-eight, she got a job instructing foreign students in English. Soon after that she began working at Denison

House, a settlement house for immigrants and their children.

At the settlement house, Amelia directed the evening school for foreign-born adults. She later said, "The people I met at Denison House were as interesting as any I have ever known." Two years later, Amelia gave up her teaching job and became a full-time social worker at Denison House. She was in charge of the classes for preschool children and girls from five to fourteen years old.

The children liked Amelia, especially when they found out that she was a flyer. They asked her many questions about airplanes. Amelia enjoyed the children and was patient with them.

While living in California, the Earharts had taken in boarders to make extra money. Amelia became close friends with one, a man named Sam Chapman. When Amelia and her mother moved to Boston, Sam moved, too. Amelia and Sam went on picnics with Muriel and her friend Albert Morrissey, whom she later married. The family thought that someday Amelia and Sam would marry. But Amelia didn't want to give up flying or her job at Denison House for marriage. Sam understood that Amelia needed to be free to pursue a career. They never married, but they always remained good friends.

There had been many advances in aviation since the Wright brothers' flight. In May 1927, Charles Lindbergh became the first man to fly across the Atlantic Ocean. Lindbergh became an idol, and the United States went aviation mad. Soon the race was on to see who would be the first woman to fly across the Atlantic.

Although women pilots had won races and set records, none of the new commercial passenger airlines would hire them. They didn't think women flyers were as capable as the men pilots who had been trained during World War I. To prove their worth, women were forced to do mostly stunt and exhibition flying. At least four women attempted to fly across the Atlantic, as passengers of male pilots, but all the women and the crews were killed making the treacherous journey.

It is likely Amelia, too, thought about crossing the Atlantic. In her free time she went flying every chance she had. She also worked with Ruth Nichols, another flyer who was trying to organize women pilots into an association. Once she even judged a model airplane tournament. Of these activities, Amelia said, "None of this was what you could call important—except to me. It was sheer fun. And it did keep me in touch with flying."

One afternoon in April 1928, while Amelia was working at Denison House, she received a phone call from a Captain Hilton H. Railey.

Amelia had never heard of him. He asked her if she would be willing to do something dangerous for aviation. Amelia wanted to know what she would have to do. The captain said he couldn't tell her yet.

She agreed to come to his office that evening to talk. The rest of the day went slowly for Amelia. Why had Captain Railey called her?

When they met, Railey told Amelia he was a publicity man. He knew that Amelia had over five hundred hours of flying time and had owned two planes. He thought she might be the right person for a secret mission.

What was the secret mission?

Captain Railey told her of an American woman living in England who had planned to fly the Atlantic Ocean in a plane called the *Friendship*. The purpose of the flight was to show friendship between America and England. When the owner's family heard that four women had died trying to fly the Atlantic, they said it was too dangerous for her to go. She agreed. But she still wanted an American woman to be the first woman to cross the Atlantic. She was looking for the right person to take her place.

"I may as well lay my cards on the table," Captain Railey finally said. "Would you fly the Atlantic?"

Amelia thought a minute. "Yes, if . . ."

"There are still many 'ifs'," Captain Railey said, "so don't begin on yours."

Amelia liked the idea of being the first woman to cross the Atlantic. She wasn't afraid. Captain Railey told her she would have to go to New York and get the approval of three men: the plane owner's lawyer, the owner's brother, John Phipps, and George Putnam, a publisher.

A few weeks later, Amelia went to George Putnam's office to meet with the men. Putnam was the publisher of Charles A. Lindbergh's story of his solo flight from New York to Paris. Now he wanted to publish the story of the first woman to fly across the Atlantic.

Amelia was told that the sponsor of the flight was Mrs. Amy Guest of London. The pilot would be Wilmer "Bill" Stultz, and the navigator-mechanic Lou "Slim" Gordon. Amelia would only be a passenger. She was disappointed. She wanted to pilot the plane, at least some of the time. But she hadn't yet learned to fly with instruments, and she lacked experience with large planes. As official recorder for the flight, she would keep the logbook, a daily diary of what happened on the trip. Although it mattered to Amelia, it didn't matter to Mrs. Guest or to the publicity people that the first woman to cross the Atlantic in a plane wouldn't actually be flying it. They thought it would be enough of an accomplishment just for her to ride along.

Amelia left New York not knowing if she had been approved. But a few days later she was told the flight was hers.

Amelia eagerly looked forward to her "great adventure," as she called it. The project was so secret, however, she wasn't allowed to tell anyone. Even her family didn't know that Amelia was planning to fly across the Atlantic Ocean.

Because there were more than three thousand miles to fly over water, the *Friendship* was being made over into a seaplane. The wheels of the plane were replaced with pontoons so it could float. The fuselage, or body of the ship, was painted bright orange, a color that would attract attention if the plane crashed in the ocean.

Bill and Slim tested the *Friendship* many times. But to keep her part in the project secret, Amelia never went to the hangar in the East Boston Airport. She worked at Denison House as usual.

There were rumors that two other women were secretly getting ready to fly the Atlantic. Because the publicity people for the *Friendship* wanted their flight to beat the others, they told the mechanics to hurry. The *Friendship* must be the first plane with a woman aboard to cross the Atlantic.

Amelia knew how dangerous the flight was. While waiting for the plane to be prepared, she wrote a farewell letter to Muriel. In it she said, ". . . If I succeed, all will be well. If I don't, I shall be happy to pop off in the midst of such an adventure."

When the plane was finally ready, the flight was delayed because of weather. There was either too much fog or too little wind. Conditions had to be just right in Boston and over the Atlantic.

On June 3, 1928, the *Friendship* finally prepared for takeoff from Boston Harbor. Bill turned the plane into the wind and began the long run. Amelia held her breath while the engines started. But the *Friendship* was too heavy to rise from the water.

The pilots dropped six cans of gas overboard. Bill taxied back and turned into the wind again. He began the run, but the plane still wouldn't lift into the air. Lou Gower, the extra pilot who was on board in case of an emergency, moved to the back of the plane to help balance it.

Once more Bill headed into the wind. Again the motors strained and the plane ran forward, but again it couldn't lift off. There was still too much weight. It was decided that Lou would leave the plane in a small boat.

As Lou boarded the boat, Bill shook his head. He told Slim and Amelia that he didn't think the *Friendship* would ever get off. Amelia wouldn't believe it. The *Friendship* had to fly!

Bill turned the plane into the wind once again. The *Friendship* was off at last!

3 Amelia the Pilot

Just before the *Friendship* left Boston Harbor, the lock on the cabin door broke. Although Slim tied a heavy gasoline can to the door to keep it closed, during takeoff a strong wind forced the door to swing open. Amelia noticed the can moving toward the door. She jumped for the cord, pulled the door closed, and yelled for Slim. He began working on the lock.

Suddenly the door swung out again, and Slim lost his balance. The *Friendship* was flying two thousand feet above the sea. Slim would die if he fell out. At the last second, he lurched away from the open door. Safe!

Meanwhile, the gasoline can began to roll across the floor. Amelia flung her arms around the can and rolled with it. She, too, was almost at the open door before she stopped the can. Slim pulled on the cord and finally managed to close the door. Amelia sat up on the floor and exchanged grins with Slim. He tied the door shut with a strip of strong leather and fastened it firmly around a wooden support in the cabin.

After that, Amelia wished she could sit down and relax, but there were no passenger seats. Although it was June, the cabin was cold. The only heater was in the open cockpit where the men were seated. Amelia was glad she'd borrowed a warm, fur-lined flying suit. It covered her completely from head to toe, shoes and all. To be nearer the heater, she knelt behind the cockpit, between the gasoline cans and the table for navigational instruments.

As soon as the plane took off, George Putnam and Captain Railey called a news conference and told the world that a woman named Amelia Earhart was flying to England. That day the *Christian Science Monitor* ran a story and photo of Amelia. The caption read, "She has the Lindbergh look."

People saw Amelia's resemblance to Lindbergh at once, especially when she wore flying togs. The two flyers looked somewhat alike, and both were slim with short, curly hair. Amelia, like Lindbergh, was also modest, publicity-shy, and dedicated to aviation. Later, when people called her "Lady Lindy," she apologized to Mrs. Lindbergh for the "ridiculous publicity." Amelia felt she hadn't done anything to earn the famous nickname.

In those days, planes could not carry enough fuel to make nonstop flights. The *Friendship* was scheduled to fly up the New England coast and refuel in Newfoundland. Because of dense fog the plane only made it to Halifax, Nova Scotia. Reporters came to the hotel in Halifax where the crew was staying. They wanted to talk to Amelia. The first woman to attempt to fly over the Atlantic Ocean was news. She tried to dodge their questions, but at breakfast she had her picture taken with Bill and Slim and talked briefly to the news people. When the plane left Halifax, Amelia was glad to leave the reporters behind.

The next stop was Trepassey Bay, Newfoundland. There was a holiday spirit as the plane landed on the water. Everyone who read the papers or listened to the radio knew of the *Friendship*'s flight. It seemed to Amelia that the entire town of Trepassey had come out to cheer them. "It is just like a rodeo," she said. Dozens of small boats circled the plane, and it seemed as if every boatman wanted to throw the rope that would tie the *Friendship* to its mooring.

Finally, the boats left. The *Friendship*'s crew only intended to stay in Trepassey for two or three days, but because of bad weather they couldn't take off for almost two weeks. While they were waiting, Amelia received a telegram from Putnam. He signed it *G.P.* From then on Amelia called George Putnam "G.P." She answered the telegram and signed it *A.E.* After that, everyone called her "A.E." She liked *A.E.* better than *Amelia* or her other nicknames.

On Sunday, June 17, Bill tried several times to take off. The crew dumped everything that wasn't necessary for the flight, including two hundred gallons of emergency gasoline, a raft, and life preservers. They took very little food along—only a few egg sandwiches, oranges, chocolate, and some emergency rations. The men had a small thermos of coffee, while Amelia brought only water.

At 11:00 A.M., the *Friendship* took off. It soon climbed to three thousand feet and leveled off. For hours it flew through a wet, gray sky. Then, because it was foggy, Bill decided to take the plane higher where he thought they'd find better weather. Instead they ran into a snowstorm. The plane shook and shivered so hard Bill had to nose it down again.

Flying low, there was a strong head wind to buck, and minutes later it began to rain. The *Friendship* flew all night at a speed of 106 miles per hour. The cabin was as dark as the inside of a closet. Slim shined the flashlight on the compass for Bill to read. Amelia could barely see her logbook, but she kept writing in it. She held her left thumb in the place where each line started so she would know where to begin again.

At 3:15 A.M., Amelia wrote in her log that she could see dawn to the left. In the northern latitude in which they were flying, it was light until 10:00 P.M., and dawn appeared around 3:00 A.M.

The fog and bumpy air continued. Bill took the plane to eleven thousand feet to climb over a bank of clouds. The extra altitude didn't help; there was only more fog and bumpy air. Bill checked the gasoline. There was only enough fuel for about six more hours, so he decided not to climb any higher and waste gas. He took the plane into a steep dive through the clouds. Amelia felt a sharp pain in her ears. She wrote in the log, "We are going down. Probably Bill is going through. Fog is lower here, too. Haven't hit it yet, but soon will so far as I can see from the back window . . . . Everything shut out."

Bill tried the radio, but it had been silent since 8:00 P.M. and was still

Amelia Earhart, 1903.

Graduation from Ogontz School, Philadelphia, 1918.

In nurses's aide uniform.

In a training plane, Boston, 1926.

Meeting the lady mayor of Southampton, England, after flight across the Atlantic, 1928.

Arrival in Ireland after solo transatlantic flight, 1932.

Amelia Earhart Putnam and George Palmer Putnam, 1936.

Amelia and her mother after Amelia's solo flight from Hawaii to California, 1935.

Selecting trophy for the 1936 Women's Air Race.

With flight crew, Miami, May 31, 1937.

out of order. He had been flying completely on instruments.

Amelia wrote, "Instrument flying. Slow descent first. Going down fast. It takes a lot to make my ears hurt. Five thousand now. Awfully wet. Water dripping in window."

Just before 8:00 A.M., according to Slim's calculations, the *Friendship* should have sighted Ireland. But there was no sign of land.

Suddenly a big transatlantic ocean liner appeared out of the fog. The ship should have been going in the same direction as the *Friendship*, but instead it was going across the plane's path. Was the *Friendship* off course? Were they lost?

Bill dropped down and circled the ship. He wanted the captain to paint his bearings on the deck so the *Friendship* could see them from the air. How would they get the captain's attention without a radio?

Amelia wrote a note asking what the ship's position was. She put it in a paper bag with two oranges for weight. She aimed it at the deck through the hatch. It missed and fell into the sea!

The crew had to decide quickly. They couldn't circle forever. If their course was wrong, wouldn't it be wise to land in the water and be hauled aboard the ship? They'd be safe and sound, but their flight would be over. There wouldn't be enough fuel to take off again and make it to England. Or should they continue in the direction they were going and hope to reach England? They decided not to give up. There was still about enough gas to fly for two hours, and it seemed best to use it to get them to England. They continued to fly eastward.

At 8:50 A.M., London time, the weary *Friendship* crew was relieved to sight two little boats. But relief turned to anxiety when Slim said that according to the direction the boats were going, the *Friendship* was definitely off course. Soon another ship appeared out of the fog. It, too, was cutting across the *Friendship*'s path. The name on the ship's side was the *America*.

Amelia wrote in her logbook, ". . . One hour's gas. Mess. All craft cutting our course. Why?"

But there was no turning back now. Before they went on, Amelia lay on her stomach and took a picture of the *America*. It was the first photo ever taken of a ship at sea from a plane.

Bill headed the plane down to five hundred feet. A short while later, Slim let out a yell. He'd spotted land in the distance. What a welcome sight!

Islands appeared below. The fuel was almost gone. Hurriedly, Bill chose a safe place to bring the plane in and made a perfect landing.

The flyers were surprised to learn that they had flown clear across Ireland, and although they'd been scheduled to land at Southampton, England, they'd landed at Burry Port, Wales, about 140 miles to the northwest. The boats the *Friendship* had flown over were not traveling parallel to it because they had been crossing the Irish Sea rather than the Atlantic Ocean.

Bill taxied to a buoy a half mile offshore, and Slim tied the plane. They had flown across the Atlantic! The trip had taken twenty hours and forty minutes.

Since they weren't expected in Wales, nobody was waiting for them. Slim crawled out on a pontoon and shouted loudly to attract attention. Amelia waved a white towel out of the open window of the. cockpit. Nothing happened except that a man on shore took off his coat and waved back.

At last some policemen rowed out. They arranged for another boat to take the flyers to shore. News of the *Friendship*'s arrival spread. Thousands of Welshmen came to the dock to welcome them. The townspeople couldn't believe that the *Friendship* had flown all the way from America— three thousand miles!

"Amelia! Amelia!" they cheered. She made a speech giving Bill the

credit for piloting the plane. The crowd didn't want to hear about Bill. Amelia was the one they wanted to see and touch. Amelia was the one who had to sign autograph after autograph.

Later, the people of Burry Port, Wales, put up a monument that said, "Erected in commemoration of Miss Amelia Earhart of Boston, U.S.A., the first woman to fly over the Atlantic Ocean. Also of her companions, Wilmer Stultz and Louis Gordon. Flew from Trepassey, Newfoundland, to Burry Port, in twenty hours and forty minutes in the seaplane *Friendship* on June 18, 1928."

From Wales, the crew flew to Southampton, England, to meet Mrs.

Guest, the sponsor of the flight, the lady mayor, and other important citizens of Southampton. Then it was on to London, where there were two weeks of teas, parties, newspaper interviews, and speeches. Amelia even received a cable of congratulations from President Calvin Coolidge.

In England, Amelia bought a sports plane from Lady Mary Heath, a famous aviator. The plane was an Avro Avian. It was small and light, much like Amelia's first yellow Kinner.

Anything Amelia said or did in England was news. She kept insisting that she was about as important "as a sack of potatoes" on the *Friendship* flight. She told everyone that Bill Stultz deserved all the credit.

Amelia was glad when they boarded a ship and left for home. But when they arrived in New York, she was again the center of attention. She got the same warm welcome New Yorkers had given Lindbergh only a year before. Cheering admirers lined the streets and leaned out of office-building windows to catch a glimpse of the celebrity as she rode on the folded canvas top of a convertible to City Hall. Horns blasted and church bells rang out as people screamed her name and pelted her roadster with a snowstorm of torn telephone books, ticker tape, and confetti. Mayor Jimmy Walker presented Amelia with a key to the city.

Amelia was overwhelmed with her welcome. More and more people called her "Lady Lindy." She tried to tell them she didn't deserve the nickname because she had only been a passenger on the flight across the Atlantic. They were too excited to listen.

In America thousands of letters, telegrams, and invitations were waiting for Amelia. The *Friendship*'s crew was invited to visit thirty-two cities. "If we accepted all the invitations," Amelia said, "I might not have got home for a year and a day!" On advice from G.P., the flyers visited only five other cities. They were given medals at each one. But Amelia was relieved when the tour was over and she could get home. She wanted to spend time with her family.

Because of all the publicity, Amelia received many job offers. She was asked to write newspaper articles and appear in magazine ads. G.P. gave her a contract to write a book about the *Friendship*'s flight.

In a short while, Amelia earned $50,000. Although she hadn't officially received a penny for the flight, the trip had paid off. Amelia planned to use the money to pay for her future flights. She was famous, but being a passenger meant nothing. She wanted to prove she was a *pilot*. She wanted to show the world that women were important to aviation.

At G.P.'s urging, Amelia wrote her book *20 Hours and 40 Minutes* at the Putnam home. She had a talent for writing, and her book was a great success. She dedicated it to Dorothy Binney Putnam, G.P.'s wife.

Amelia liked to write, but she wanted to get back to flying. She couldn't wait to try out her new plane. In September 1928, she planned a vacation flying from coast to coast—alone. She would take her time getting to Los Angeles, then visit friends and her father, who had remarried, and attend the National Air Races there. She called this kind of trip "vagabonding in the air."

Using several navigation maps, Amelia made a simple flight plan for the first part of her journey. When she got out west she intended to buy more maps and plan the last leg of the flight in more detail. She took off from a Rye, New York, polo field with her map pinned to her dress. Although Amelia usually wore slacks and a jacket when she flew, on this trip she wore a dress to show that women didn't need any special clothing to fly.

Bad luck struck from the beginning. Landing in Pittsburgh for gas, the little Avian turned completely over and the propeller splintered. Although Amelia was upside down, held by her safety belt, she was able to switch off the engine. She climbed out without a scratch.

The plane was repaired and Amelia was off again. She flew over many towns—Dayton, Terre Haute, St. Louis. From the air they all looked alike. How she wished their names were painted on flat roofs in large white or yellow letters so pilots could see them!

Flying west from Ft. Worth, Amelia ran into bad weather. The plane swayed and lurched. She couldn't keep it level. Wind tore at the map pinned to her dress. The gas tank was almost empty. Amelia wrote later, "Through particularly bumpy going, while I tried to fly and also to pump gas from the reserve into the gravity tank, I lost my map." She had to make an emergency landing, even if she didn't know where she was.

Amelia saw a busy highway and followed it. She flew over a small town and saw a deserted street. Although unpaved, it was smooth and open enough for her to land. The people of Hobbs, New Mexico, were surprised to see an airplane parked on their main street! They all came out to see what Amelia looked like.

Back in the air again, Amelia kept going. After making several forced landings to fix flat tires and replace engine parts, she finally arrived in Los Angeles. She visited her father and attended the air races, then made the return trip east. On the way back she had more engine trouble and once again had to make a forced landing, this time in a farmer's field in Utah. At last, in late October 1928, Amelia's cross-country trip was completed. She had set another record. She was the first woman to fly across the continent and back, alone!

Amelia was living in New York with her mother when *Cosmopolitan* magazine offered her a job as aviation editor. She said, "With Cosmo's enormous circulation I welcomed the opportunity to reach a great audience with my favorite subject." She became a staff member and wrote many articles about flying. Acting as Amelia's advisor and manager, G.P. arranged her first lecture tour. From then on, she lectured nonstop at universities, women's clubs, and other groups.

Amelia was very much in demand. She tried her best to convince people that flying was safe. When she lectured, she wore high-heeled shoes and dresses, sometimes those she had designed herself. Often when she spoke to women's clubs, her mother went along.

Now that she was so involved with aviation, Amelia realized that she'd never again be a social worker. She missed Denison House and the children, but she was no longer flying just for fun. Aviation was her life.

Amelia didn't think of herself as a leader, but other people did. She answered thousands of letters from young girls who looked up to her as an example of the kind of woman they would like to become. They wanted her advice on how to learn to fly. They asked her to convince their parents flying was safe, and they wanted to know how to persuade colleges to include flying courses as part of their curricula.

Amelia sold her Avro Avian and bought a much larger, used Lockheed Vega. In July 1929, on her way to the first Women's Air Derby in Santa Monica, California, she stopped at the Lockheed factory in California to have her Vega inspected. It was in such bad shape that the Lockheed management traded her a new plane for the broken-down one.

The first Women's Air Derby was a major event at the 1929 National Air Races. The twenty leading women pilots of the day were in the cross-country race. Newspapers called them "petticoat pilots" and "flying flappers." Men laughed at the "Powder Puff Derby." They thought women were not suited to handle planes as well as men. They were wrong.

When the race began on August 18, Amelia's brand-new Lockheed was lined up with the other racing planes. The women were given eight days to fly across the United States to Cleveland, Ohio. The first-place prize was $25,000.

It was a dangerous race. One woman was killed, and many had engine trouble or ran out of gas. But of the twenty pilots who had started, fifteen flew their planes to Cleveland. Amelia finished third.

After the race, a group of women flyers formed an association. It was called the "Ninety-Nines" because there were ninety-nine original members, all licensed pilots. Amelia was the first president. In time, the Ninety Nines became an international association, and it is still in existence today.

Later that year at Los Angeles, Amelia set the new speed record for women over a one-mile distance. On June 28, 1930, at Detroit, she established the international speed record for women over a one-hundred-kilometer course. From then on, Amelia kept setting records. She wanted to show the public that a woman could be an outstanding pilot.

In addition to her writing, lectures, and flying, Amelia took care of money matters for her mother and also kept in touch with her father until he died in September 1930.

Perhaps after her father's death, Amelia took a look at her own life. She had no regrets for how she'd lived. But something was missing. She had sinusitis again, and perhaps she thought of going home to rest. But where was home? Certainly not the room she now shared with her secretary in a New York City women's hotel. If she was married, she'd have a home.

Amelia had often said marriage was a cage, and that she would rather work or fly than have a husband. Her friend Sam Chapman had asked her to marry him, but Amelia had turned him down. G.P., who was now divorced, had proposed five times. Each time she had refused him, too. He remained her manager, advising her about jobs and money matters. When, for the sixth time, G.P. asked Amelia to marry him, she surprised everyone by saying yes. Amelia was thirty-three years old, and G.P. was forty-five.

Amelia Mary Earhart and George Palmer Putnam were married at G.P.'s mother's home on February 7, 1931. The newlyweds made their home in Rye, New York.

Their marriage was an unusual partnership for the 1930s. G.P. believed as Amelia did that women should work after marriage if they wanted to. G.P. and Amelia respected each other's right to privacy, and for the most part Mr. and Mrs. George Putnam went their separate ways. Amelia spent many hours alone reading and writing romantic poetry and speeches on aviation, women's rights, and the brutality of war.

G.P. was a tall, good-looking man. Full of energy, he always had several things going at once. He was a member of a rich and famous publishing family, and he had developed good business sense. He was also the author of ten books.

Amelia was modest and quiet, and G.P. was just the opposite. Some people thought he was pushy. He probably deserves the credit for making Amelia popular with the public. He always introduced her as "Miss Earhart." The average American knew G.P. only as Amelia's husband.

Amelia's next flying adventure was in an autogiro, an aircraft similar to a helicopter. After being a passenger in a autogiro for only twenty minutes, Amelia soloed in it, using her knowledge of airplanes to figure out how it operated. When she landed, she said, "I don't know if I flew it or it flew me!" But a few days later, she took an autogiro to 18,415 feet, setting a new altitude record for autogiros.

While giving an autogiro demonstration at a state fair in Detroit one day, Amelia lived through another crash. G.P. watched Amelia's autogiro rise above the trees. Suddenly it plummeted to the ground. Quickly G.P. jumped a fence and ran to help his wife. He tripped over a wire, fell, and cracked several ribs. Amelia came out of the accident unhurt. She laughingly told G.P. that it was safer to fly than to be on the ground.

Because she had only been a passenger on the *Friendship* flight, Amelia never wanted to accept credit for it. She planned to solo across the Atlantic as soon as she had enough experience. In 1932 she decided she was ready.

Exactly five years to the day after Lindbergh's famous flight, Amelia set off and became the first woman to fly the Atlantic Ocean alone. For weeks she had studied weather and practiced navigating by instruments. On May 20, 1932, Amelia left New Jersey and flew to Harbor Grace, Newfoundland, where she planned to leave for her Atlantic hop. That evening, Amelia took off for Paris. She was alone in the plane, the way she liked best to fly.

The weather turned bad just before midnight. The hands of her altimeter spun wildly, and the device broke. In twelve years of piloting, this had never happened to Amelia. Now there was no way of knowing how high she was flying. A few minutes later, lightning zig-zagged across the sky and thunder boomed. Rain hit the outside of the plane with sharp rapid beats. Then the rain began to freeze. Ice formed on the wings. The Lockheed made a sudden downward plunge and went into a spin. Several other instruments broke.

Amelia righted the spinning plane and held it level. The warmth at the lower altitude melted the ice. She wrote later, "Through the blackness below I could see the whitecaps too close for comfort." Amelia climbed again, guessing her altitude.

Four hours into the flight, Amelia looked out and saw flames leaking out of a crack in the engine exhaust pipe. At dawn she was between two

cloud layers. She flew on for ten hours. Now the exhaust pipe was vibrating badly. There were about two hours of the flight left to go. Switching on the reserve tanks, Amelia found that a line leading to the fuel gauge was leaking. Fumes were escaping into the cockpit.

With broken instruments, a loose exhaust pipe, and a gasoline leak, Amelia knew she couldn't risk flying all the way to Paris. Her engine might not hold out. The gas fumes were now so strong she was barely able to take a deep breath. She turned the plane in the direction of what she thought was Ireland.

She sighted land. There was a railroad below. Amelia followed it to a big city, but she could not find an airfield. She had to fly to the city outskirts and put the Lockheed down in a pasture, scaring the cows. She had landed in Londonderry, Ireland.

Amelia had made it! She was the first woman to pilot a plane across the Atlantic Ocean alone. She wasn't "only as important as a sack of potatoes" this time. Now the world knew that a woman could handle an airplane as well as a man. She felt that all women flyers shared in her victory. Later, when Amelia was honored in London, Rome, and Brussels, she enjoyed the fuss made over her. She felt she had earned it.

At home, President Herbert Hoover invited her to the White House and gave her a medal. She received other medals from various clubs and societies all over the United States.

It wasn't long before Amelia began to think about another flight. This time she planned to fly across the Pacific Ocean. She bought a new red Lockheed Vega for the trip. She and G.P. sailed to Honolulu just before Christmas 1934, and on January 11, 1935, Amelia flew alone from Honolulu, Hawaii, to Oakland, California. It took her a little over eighteen hours. In Oakland, thousands of cheering people greeted her. As tired as she was, she couldn't help smiling. She had one more amazing record to add to her long list. Now she was the first person to solo anywhere in the Pacific and the first person to solo over both the Atlantic and Pacific oceans. There could be no doubt in anyone's mind that Amelia Earhart was an outstanding pilot.

During the rest of 1935, Amelia set even more records. In April, she made the first solo nonstop flight from Burbank, California, to Mexico City. When she arrived in Mexico City, she was given a medal in the name of Mexican women. Just a few weeks later, Amelia made the first nonstop solo flight from Mexico City to Newark, New Jersey. She didn't follow expert advice and go the long way by land. Instead, she took a more dangerous route across the waters of the Gulf of Mexico, thereby shortening her flying time and adding one more record to her long list. When she arrived in Newark, a police squad had to rescue her from her screaming admirers.

At Purdue University, Amelia was appointed a part-time advisor for women students and a consultant to the faculty of the new aviation department. Each year she was to spend a month in residence at Purdue. Amelia encouraged coeds to prepare for any career they liked. She didn't believe that women should be allowed to do only certain kinds of work.

The university set up the Amelia Earhart Research Foundation. In April 1936, money from the fund was used to buy Amelia a plane. It was a Lockheed Electra, the newest and best nonmilitary plane in the world. Amelia was delighted. She described the plane as "simply elegant." When she took official possession of the plane, she said to the president and trustees of Purdue University, "My ambition is to have this wonderful gift produce practical results for the future of commercial flying and for the women who may want to fly tomorrow's planes."

The Lockheed had all the latest aviation innovations, including a two-way radio. The plane's top speed was two hundred miles per hour. Because it was a twin-engine, ten-passenger plane, Amelia had plenty of space for extra equipment.

Amelia was to use the Electra for research. The university and Lockheed wanted to find ways to build better planes. Amelia herself wondered whether time and money should be spent to develop bigger and faster planes or planes that were safer.

Amelia was almost thirty-nine years old now. She got along well with G.P. There was enough money to do the things she wanted. She'd received the Distinguished Flying Cross—the first woman ever to do so. She'd won medals and honors and set many records. People recognized her mop of short, curly hair and her famous grin. They thought of her as an outstanding American woman.

After setting so many records, many other people would have retired and lived an easy life. But Amelia was never one to watch life go by. She always made things happen. There were rumors that she was planning another flight. She had crossed the Atlantic, bridged the Gulf of Mexico, and flown the Pacific from Hawaii to California. What was left for her to do?

When reporters questioned her, she said, "I'm nearly sold on the idea of flying around the world. But I'm a busy person this year."

Three months later, when reporters again asked Amelia about her plans, she said, "Well, I'm going to try to fly around the world. I'm going to make it as near the equator as I can—about 27,000 miles. I'll fly east to west." Circling the globe near the equator would be a dangerous and difficult trip, especially because of the long, uncharted expanse of water that the Electra, a land plane, must fly over. Amelia knew the plan was risky. Although a few pilots had followed a shorter route north of the equator, no man or woman had ever circled the earth at its midsection. Piloting a plane around the world would be Amelia Earhart's greatest triumph.

4 What Happened to Amelia?

Preparations for Amelia's around-the-world flight took almost a year. The Electra went through many changes at the Lockheed factory. Extra fuel tanks, a large chart table, and special windows were put in. Unlike the *Friendship*, the Electra did not have pontoons. It was thought that pontoons would slow it down.

Arrangements had to be made for fuel stops along the way. The United States State Department helped Amelia get permission to land in foreign countries.

In the Putnams' new California home, Amelia pored over the maps and charts. She wanted to be well prepared. The weather, mountains, and landing fields worried her. Very often she would have to rely on instruments. Her instruments and radio were the best available, but they were primitive compared to modern equipment.

Finally, Amelia, her crew, the Electra, and the charts were ready. Mechanics with spare parts waited at airports around the world in case repairs were needed. Amelia, who always said she'd rather fly alone, had the largest crew she'd ever flown with. Paul Mantz, a pilot, would fly with her from Oakland, California, to Hawaii. Then Fred Noonan and Harry Manning, two expert navigators, would take Mantz's place and direct her to Howland Island, where she would refuel. Howland was just a tiny spot in the Pacific Ocean. Amelia needed all the help she could get to land there safely. Manning would continue on with her to Australia.

On the morning of March 17, 1937, the Electra was ready for takeoff. While they waited for the rainy weather to clear, a reporter asked Amelia the often-repeated question, "Why are you making this flight?" She answered, "Because I want to." She had told her friends, "I think I have one last long-distance flight left in me, and this is it."

About 4:30 P.M., the sun came out. Without telling reporters she was taking off, Amelia climbed into the cockpit. The Electra roared down the runway and headed for Honolulu.

A photographer in a plane took a picture as the Electra flew over the Golden Gate Bridge. Many newspapers ran the photo.

Less than sixteen hours after leaving Oakland, the Electra landed in Honolulu. Everything had gone well. Because it was raining, the plane was moved to a longer concrete runway at another field. The engines were refueled and tested. Again Amelia waited for better weather.

The next day the weather cleared. Before dawn, Amelia went to the field. Mantz put a lei of paper orchids around her neck and said goodbye. He was leaving the flight. Amelia and her navigators got into the plane. The Electra headed down the wet runway. At once, Amelia knew something was wrong. They had not picked up enough speed to take off.

One wing dropped, and the plane began to sway to the right. Amelia tried to steady it, but the right landing gear collapsed, and she lost control. She turned off the ignition just before the plane spun off the runway, smashing the landing gear and wing. Gasoline poured out of the damaged wing tanks. Because of Amelia's quick thinking there was no fire, but the shiny new Electra was a crumpled heap.

Sirens screamed as an ambulance and fire trucks raced toward the plane. Manning, Noonan, and then Amelia climbed out unhurt but badly shaken. Amelia looked pale and sad. Paul Mantz, who had stayed to watch them take off, put his arm around her shoulders. A reporter

asked Amelia, "Will you give up the flight now?" She answered quickly, "No, the flight is still on. Of course I'll be back. I want to try again."

The Electra and her crew left for California by ship. The wrecked plane was taken to the Lockheed factory to be repaired. Engineers said it would take from five weeks to two months before the plane would be ready to fly, and repairs would be costly. But Amelia was determined not to give up. She said, "Despite these troubles, there seem to me many reasons for trying to complete the flight."

The long delay for repairs meant that weather conditions around the world would be changed before Amelia could begin again. It would be especially dangerous to fly over the Caribbean in the middle of the rainy season. Amelia decided to reverse her flight plan in order to fly over the Caribbean in the first lap of the trip. She would fly to Miami for final repairs. Then she'd go west to east—from Miami to Oakland—along the equator, or as close to it as possible.

Not only were plane repairs costly, but it was expensive to change landing sites and send fuel, spare parts, and mechanics to new places. Many of Amelia's friends gave money to help pay all these expenses.

Meanwhile, Harry Manning dropped out of the flight. Fred Noonan agreed to be the navigator for the entire trip. Amelia spent a great deal of time talking to Lockheed engineers and government officials. She prepared new charts and worked out navigation problems with Fred.

Amelia's plane had a radio transmitter and receiver designed to operate on standard aviation frequencies as well as on a long-range international emergency wavelength. A trailing antenna at least two hundred fifty feet long was required for the emergency wavelength.

On May 24, Amelia and Fred were off to Miami. There mechanics spent a week putting the plane in final shape. Amelia did her share, getting dirty and greasy along with the men. The technicians couldn't get the radio to work properly and told Amelia that the long antenna was causing the trouble. They said she didn't need it, so Amelia left the antenna for the emergency wavelength in Miami.

G.P. came to Miami to wish Amelia luck. At last, just before 6:00 A.M. of June 1, 1937, the Electra eased upward into the sky.

During the next month, Amelia and Fred made an amazing journey. They flew from Miami to South America, across South America to Natal, Brazil, and from there nineteen-hundred miles across the South Atlantic Ocean to Dakar, Africa. From Dakar they headed to Gao, at the edge of the Sahara Desert, and then across the treacherous Sahara itself. After resting in the governor's home—a former sultan's palace—in Chad, French Equatorial Africa, they made their way to Karachi, India, where they took time to sight-see and ride a camel. Then on to Bangkok, Thailand; Singapore; Bandung, on the island of Java; and Darwin, Australia.

Throughout the trip Amelia wrote down her observations and sent them to G.P. and the *New York Herald Tribune*. Several times she was able to talk to G.P. by telephone.

On June 30 or July 1, New Guinea time, after flying twenty-two thousand miles from Australia, the Electra arrived at Lae, New Guinea. They had been traveling for thirty days. There were only about seven thousand miles to go.

The Electra had performed well on the hazardous trip. Except for a few minor mechanical problems, the flyers had experienced no difficulties.

The next lap of the flight would be the longest and most dangerous. Amelia had chosen a route no one had ever flown before. From Lae, she was to fly more than twenty-five hundred miles over open water before landing on little Howland Island.

Howland Island is only about two miles long and one-half mile wide—just a tiny speck in a great big ocean. If Fred and Amelia miscalculated their position by only one degree on the compass, they would miss Howland by more than forty miles. Since the Electra was not a seaplane, Amelia had to be right on target when she landed.

To lighten the plane, Fred and Amelia repacked it, throwing away everything that wasn't absolutely necessary. At about 10:00 A.M. on July 2, New Guinea time, the Electra raced down the narrow Lae jungle airstrip and lifted off.

Two Navy ships were stationed in lonely stretches of ocean to guide

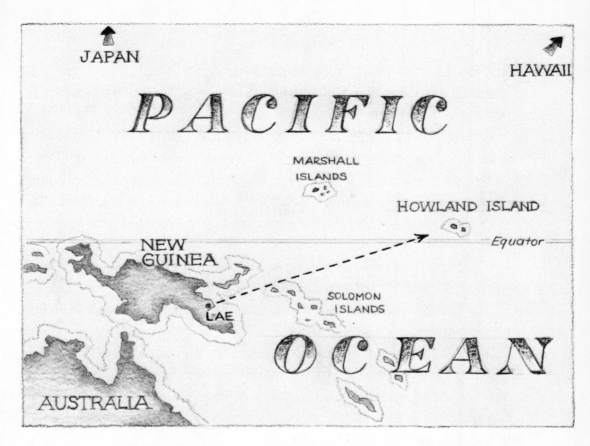

Amelia. The U.S.S. *Ontario* was halfway between Lae and Howland. The U.S.S. *Swan* was halfway between Howland and Honolulu.

The United States Coast Guard cutter *Itasca* was standing off Howland. Signals sent through the Electra's radio gear could be picked up aboard the *Itasca*. While the aviators used their own direction finder to pinpoint the island, the *Itasca* could determine the plane's position. There was also an experimental high-frequency direction finder on Howland to receive Amelia's signals.

It was planned that the *Itasca* would call the Electra by voice on the hour and half hour and would also send out the Morse Code letter "A" on the emergency wavelength. From the Electra, Amelia would send out her own signal twice an hour, and Fred would send Morse Code messages.

The plan covered everything that might happen as Amelia, Fred, and the Electra flew toward Howland Island. When they landed, they'd refuel and continue on to Honolulu.

As the flyers crossed back into yesterday at the international date line, the *Itasca*'s crew settled down to wait. They expected a long, tense night. Amelia was due about 6:30 A.M. Howland time. The *Itasca*'s searchlights were ready to go on after midnight if the plane came in early. If Amelia wasn't there by dawn, the ships were to send up smoke signals to help her find the little island.

At 5:20 P.M., New Guinea time, Amelia reported to Lae that she was past the Solomon Islands and right on course. She mentioned no trouble, but after that she didn't keep to her broadcast schedule. She radioed only a few short messages all night.

At 6:15 A.M., only minutes before the Electra was to arrive at Howland, Amelia's voice came through loud and clear on the *Itasca*'s radio. She asked what her position was and whistled into the mike so they could trace the sound. Then she said she thought the Electra was about two hundred miles from Howland.

There was too much static for the *Itasca* to send a message back. On Howland, Radioman Cipriani tried to get a bearing with his direction finder, but Amelia hadn't been on the radio long enough for him to get her signal.

The *Itasca* asked Amelia to stay on the air longer, preferably on the long-range emergency wavelength, but there was no reply.

From then on, all eyes were on the sky. Amelia's arrival time came and went. But there was no Electra. And there were no messages from the plane. Everyone was uneasy. What had gone wrong with Amelia's radio?

Half an hour after Amelia's scheduled arrival time, those who were waiting were relieved to hear her on the radio. She asked the *Itasca* to place her location. She thought she was now about a hundred miles away, but she wasn't sure. The signal was strong, which meant she was nearby, but once again she left the air too soon for the Navy direction finder to figure out exactly where she was.

At 7:18 A.M., the *Itasca* called Amelia on its radio again, asking her to send messages on the emergency wavelength. Amelia didn't answer. She hadn't reported trouble, but it seemed that something was wrong with her transmitter. Radiomen on the *Itasca* didn't realize that Amelia's emergency transmitter was practically useless because the long antenna had been left in Miami.

At 7:42 A.M., almost half an hour later, Amelia's voice came in strong. "We must be on you but cannot see you," she said. "But gas is running low. Been unable to reach you by radio. We are flying at altitude one thousand feet."

The men on the *Itasca* scanned the cloudless sky. If Amelia's plane was directly above Howland, none of them could see it. They called Amelia and told her they'd received her signal. They asked her yet again to reply on the emergency wavelength. The message was repeated at 7:49 A.M.

Six minutes later, Amelia's voice came in clearly again. She said, "KHAQQ calling *Itasca*. We are circling, but cannot hear you. Go ahead on five hundred either now or on schedule time of half hour." It was obvious that she was not picking up any of the *Itasca*'s messages. Her voice sounded higher than usual and troubled.

The men in the radio shack desperately wanted to help Amelia. She was close, but where? They hoped she wouldn't try to land until she heard their signals.

A few minutes after 8:00 A.M., Amelia told them that she had heard signals from the *Itasca* for the first time, but she couldn't get a compass bearing in order to land.

The *Itasca* kept sending signals pleading with her to answer. The Electra was two hours late now. Tension mounted in the radio room. Desperately the *Itasca* called Radioman Cipriani on Howland to ask if he had determined the plane's position. He replied that he had not—his direction-finder batteries were too weak. Smoke poured out of the *Itasca*'s funnel to guide the plane. Its trail could be seen for thirty miles. But there was no plane approaching the island. There was nothing above the *Itasca* but empty blue sky and hot sun.

The next message from Amelia came through at 8:45 A.M. It was filled with static. On 3105 kilocycles she said, "We are in a line of position 157–337. Will repeat this message. We will repeat this message on 6210 kilocycles. Wait, listening on 6210 kilocycles." She sounded frantic now. "We are running north and south."

The signal was the strongest she'd sent. Surely, Amelia was close to Howland now. The men on the ship listened for the sound of the plane overhead and waited for her broadcast on 6210 kilocycles. Silence. They kept calling her. They begged her to answer. Minutes dragged by. Nothing. They listened on all wavelengths—3105, 6210, and 500 kilocycles. She didn't reply. The words at 8:45 A.M. were the last Amelia was known to speak.

Nobody knew what the message meant. "Line 157–337" was probably the plane's position report, based on Fred's observation of the sun. Perhaps Fred and Amelia were flying north and south in a search pattern,

hoping to spot Howland. It certainly seemed as if, when the message was sent, they did not know their exact location. The radiomen realized that by now Amelia had to be out of fuel. The plane had probably crashed.

The Lockheed Company had claimed that the Electra would not sink under ordinary circumstances. So the *Itasca* began to search the water near Howland, expecting to find the plane afloat in the relatively calm seas. Several U.S. Navy ships and planes joined the *Itasca* to look for Amelia, Fred, and the Electra. At first the searchers were sure that they or someone who lived on a nearby island would find the plane and crew. But no wreckage was found, and no natives on any of the islands reported seeing the plane.

After sixteen days, the Navy had to give up the search. They had covered more than 250,000 square miles of Pacific Ocean and had spent over four million dollars. Not one trace of the missing aviators or their plane had been found.

The official government statement said that the Electra had run out of fuel about two hundred miles north of Howland Island and that "Amelia Earhart and Fred Noonan were lost at sea somewhere in the mid-Pacific on July 2, 1937."

Amelia Earhart had disappeared in a faraway place. Americans had been told that her flight was extremely dangerous and that the landing on tiny Howland Island would be difficult, but they couldn't believe that she was dead. Their heroine had crashed many times and always come out without a scratch.

There were rumors that the Electra had landed near a Japanese-held island and that the aviators were captured by the Japanese. In 1937 Japanese-American relations were tense. Some Americans thought that Amelia had been sent on a secret mission for President Roosevelt to photograph the Japanese islands. It seemed easier to believe that Amelia had been taken prisoner than that she had run out of fuel and crashed.

58

G.P., frantically trying to find his wife, asked her friend the famous pilot Jacqueline Cochran to help in the search. Jacqueline, who claimed to have extrasensory perception, told G.P. that Amelia had crashed in the ocean, but she was unhurt and the Electra was afloat. She believed that Fred had a serious head injury and was in grave condition. Jacqueline gave what she thought was the exact position of the plane. Searchers combed the area but found no trace of the Electra. Jacqueline then said that she believed that the plane had sunk after three days—and her friends with it.

Amelia's mother kept up her courage during the search and for a long time clung to the belief that the flyers would be found. She pretended that Amelia was away on a trip and would be home soon. Much later she told reporters that she believed her daughter had been captured by the

Japanese and taken to Tokyo, where she lost her life. "I'm sure there was a government mission involved in the flight," she said, "for Amelia explained there were some things she could not tell me."

Even after the search was called off, there was still hope that somewhere, somehow, the flyers were alive. Rumors continued to spring up that Amelia had been seen in various places.

Within a little over two years, World War II broke out in Europe, giving the public something else to occupy its attention. After World War II, Amelia's family and friends thought that they would find out what happened to Amelia but no evidence surfaced.

Years passed, and still Amelia's mysterious disappearance was not solved. In 1960, Fred Goerner, a newspaperman, began a six-year search to find out what happened to Amelia and Fred. While researching, he found evidence that two flyers, an American man and woman, had been held captive by the Japanese on the island of Saipan. Goerner went to Saipan to search for Fred and Amelia's graves. He never found them. He discovered rusty airplane parts under the ocean, but they turned out to be from a Japanese plane.

Goerner made appointments with Navy officials who said they would talk to him about Amelia Earhart. He thought he was about to get secret information, but at the last minute they said there was nothing to tell him.

In his book *The Search for Amelia Earhart*, Goerner came to the conclusion that Amelia was on a spying mission for President Roosevelt. Goerner claimed that she was to photograph airports and naval yards, but she crashed and was taken prisoner by the Japanese.

Goerner, however, had found no proof. Eleanor Roosevelt, the wife of President Roosevelt, said before she died that she and Franklin loved Amelia too much to have sent her to her death. In 1967, classified United States Navy files were opened to "discredit books and magazine articles which claimed Miss Earhart crashed on the island of Saipan and was executed by the Japanese as a spy." The files contained no evidence that Amelia ever had any contact with the Japanese.

Today new books with theories about Amelia's disappearance continue to be published. But the mystery of what happened to Amelia Earhart may never be solved. It is most likely that Fred and Amelia crashed into the ocean about two hundred miles north of Howland Island when the Electra ran out of fuel. Poor radio equipment, especially the lack of a long antenna, may have caused the tragedy. It is very difficult to search even a small area of the ocean, and this is probably the reason the plane has never been found.

So Amelia's life ended with her mysterious disappearance. Despite the customs of her day, she had the courage to live her life the way she wanted to, exploring the skies. Because of her passion for flying and her skill as a pilot, she established records and demonstrated to the world that a woman can fly as well as a man. She was a public idol who was a responsible leader, speaking out on issues she felt strongly about—aviation, women's rights, and war.

She was a woman who made things happen, and she is still admired today.

Glossary

airstrip or **runway** a cleared or paved strip of ground for airplanes to land on and take off from.

altimeter an instrument that measures altitude above sea or ground level, usually by recording changes in air pressure.

altitude the height of an airplane above the earth's surface.

antenna a rod, wire, or set of wires used to send or receive radio waves.

autogiro an aircraft similar to a helicopter, with a free-spinning rotor, or horizontal propeller, to keep it in the air and a nose propeller to move it forward.

aviation the study, building, and operation of aircraft, especially airplanes.

cockpit the space in the body of an airplane where, depending on the size of the plane, the pilot, the pilot and crew, or the pilot, crew, and passengers sit.

controls instruments used to start, stop, and guide airplanes.

course the direction of flight of an aircraft.

direction finder a part on a radio receiver that tells the direction of incoming radio waves.

dive the steep downward plunge of an airplane at great speed.

exhaust pipe the pipe used for the escape of used and often harmful gas from the engine of an airplane.

Federal Aviation Authority an agency in the United States Department of Transportation which controls air traffic, establishes safety requirements, and certifies aircraft, airports, and pilots.

frequency number of cycles per second of electric current sent out by a radio. Radios can send messages at different frequencies.

fuel gauge an instrument used to measure the amount of fuel in a tank.

fuselage the central body of an airplane which carries the crew, passengers, and cargo.

gravity tank a fuel tank in which the flow of gasoline to an airplane's engine is controlled by gravity.

hangar an enclosed space for keeping an airplane.

head wind wind blowing opposite to the direction an airplane is moving.

idle to run an engine out of gear so that no work is performed and therefore an airplane does not move.

ignition the device that causes fuel to begin to burn in an engine.

instrument flying flying an airplane using information supplied by instruments rather than by a pilot's vision and hearing.

kilocycle one thousand cycles per second. Kilocycles are used to measure radio frequency.

landing gear wheels, pontoons, etc., under an airplane on which it rests when on land or water.

latitude the distance north or south of the earth's equator.

log or **logbook** a book for keeping the record of an airplane's flight.

loop an airplane maneuver that looks like a handwritten letter *l*.

mechanic a worker skilled with tools who repairs engines or other machines.

navigation the skill of guiding the course of airplanes.

navigator the person who directs an airplane on its course.

pilot the person who operates an aircraft.

pontoons canoe-shaped parts of an airplane used for landing on or taking off from water.

propeller a screwlike device consisting of a turning hub with blades, used to move an airplane forward.

radio receiver a device which changes electric currents or waves into signals that can be heard or seen.

radio transmitter a device that sends out signals by electric currents, or waves.

roll an airplane maneuver in which a complete lengthwise revolution is made while the plane is flying in about the same horizontal position.

seaplane an airplane that can take off from and land on water, especially an airplane with pontoons instead of wheels.

skid an airplane maneuver in which the plane slides sideways while turning.

solo an airplane flight during which the pilot is alone; to fly a plane alone.

stall the falling of an airplane which occurs when the plane is angled too sharply.

stunt flying flying an airplane with the intent of using skids, rolls, stalls, and other maneuvers as tricks.

tailspin the downward movement of an airplane with its nose first and tail spinning behind.

throttle a lever, pedal, or handle used to control the flow of gas to an engine.

Bibliography

These are some of the books and magazine articles the author studied before writing Amelia Earhart Takes Off.

Backus, Jean L. *Letters from Amelia*. Boston: Beacon Press, 1983.

Briand, Paul L., Jr. "Was She on a Secret Mission?" *Ms.*, September 1976.

Davis, Burke. *Amelia Earhart*. New York: G.P. Putnam's Sons, 1972.

Earhart, Amelia. *Last Flight*. (Arranged by George Palmer Putnam). New York: Harcourt Brace and Company, 1937.

————. *The Fun of It*. New York: Harcourt Brace and Company, 1937.

————. *20 Hrs. 40 Min*. New York: G.P. Putnam's Sons, 1928.

Goerner, Fred. *The Search for Amelia Earhart*. Garden City, New York: Doubleday and Company, Inc., 1966.

Hamill, Pete. "The Cult of Amelia Earhart," *Ms.*, September 1976.

Moolman, Valerie. *Women Aloft*. Alexandria, Virginia: Time-Life Books, 1981.

National Geographic Society. "The Society's Special Medal Awarded to Amelia Earhart," *The National Geographic Magazine*, September 1932.

Putnam, George Palmer. *Soaring Wings: A Biography of Amelia Earhart*. New York: Harcourt, Brace and Company, 1939.